Cascando

and other short dramatic pieces

Works by Samuel Beckett Published by Grove Press

Cascando and Other Short Dramatic Pieces (Words and Music;
    Eh Joe; Play; Come and Go; Film [original version])
Collected Poems in English and French
The Collected Shorter Plays of Samuel Beckett
The Collected Works of Samuel Beckett (twenty-five volumes)
Company
Disjecta
Endgame and Act Without Words
Ends and Odds (Not I; That Time; Footfalls; Ghost Trio; . . . but the
    clouds . . . ; Theatre I; Theatre II; Radio I; Radio II)
Film: A Film Script
First Love and Other Shorts (From an Abandoned Work; Enough;
    Imagination Dead Imagine; Ping; Not I; Breath)
Fizzles
Happy Days
How It Is
Ill Seen Ill Said
Krapp's Last Tape and Other Dramatic Pieces (All That Fall; Embers
    [a play for radio]; Act Without Words I and II [mimes])
The Lost Ones
Malone Dies
Mercier and Camier
Molloy
More Pricks Than Kicks
Murphy
Poems in English
Proust
Ohio Impromptu, Catastrophe, and What Where: Three Plays
Rockaby and Other Short Pieces (Ohio Impromptu; All Strange
    Away; A Piece of Monologue)
Stories and Texts for Nothing
Three Novels (Molloy; Malone Dies; The Unnamable)
Waiting for Godot
Watt
Worstward Ho

Samuel Beckett

CASCANDO

and other short dramatic pieces

Grove Press
New York

Published by Grove Press
a division of Wheatland Corporation
841 Broadway
New York, N.Y. 10003

First Evergreen Edition 1969
ISBN: 0-8021-5099-3
Library of Congress Catalog Card Number: 68-22023

Manufactured in the United States of America
This book is printed on acid-free paper.
20 19 18 17 16 15 14 13 12 11 10

Contents

Cascando

a radio play

translated from the French by the author

music by Marcel Mihalovici

OPENER (*dry as dust*): It is the month of May . . . for me.

Pause.

Yes, that's right.

Pause.

I open.

VOICE (*low, panting*):—story . . . if you could finish it . . . you could rest . . . you could sleep . . . not before . . . oh I know . . . the ones I've finished . . . thousands and one . . . all I ever did . . . in my life . . . with my life . . . saying to myself . . . finish this one . . . it's the right one . . . then rest . . . then sleep . . . no more stories . . . no more words . . . and finished it . . . and not the right one . . . couldn't rest . . . straight away another . . . to begin . . . to finish . . . saying to myself . . . finish this one . . . then rest . . . this time it's the right one . . . this time you have it . . . and finished it . . . and not the right one . . . couldn't rest . . . straight away another . . . but this one . . . it's different . . . I'll finish it . . . then rest . . . it's the right one . . . this time I have it . . . I've got it . . . Woburn . . . I resume . . . a long life . . . already . . . say what you like . . . a few misfortunes . . . that's enough . . . five years later . . . ten years . . . I don't know . . . Woburn . . . he's changed . . . not enough . . . recognizable . . . in the shed . . . yet another . . . waiting for night . . . night to fall . . . to go out . . . go on . . . elsewhere . . . sleep elsewhere . . . it's slow . . . he lifts his head . . . now and then . . . his eyes . . . to the window . . . it's darkening . . . the earth is darkening . . . it's night . . . he gets up . . . knees first . . . then up . . . on his feet . . . slips

9

out . . . Woburn . . . same old coat . . . right the sea . . . left the hills . . . he has the choice . . . he has only—

OPENER (*with* VOICE): And I close.

Silence.

I open the other.

MUSIC: . . . .

OPENER (*with* MUSIC): And I close.

Silence.

I open both.

VOICE ⎱
MUSIC ⎰ (*together*): —on . . . it's getting on . . . finish it
. . . .
. . . don't give up . . . then rest . . . sleep . . . nŏt before
. . . .
. . . finish it . . . it's the right one . . . this time you have
. . . .
it . . . you've got it . . . it's there . . . somewhere . . .
. . . .
you've got him . . . follow him . . . don't lose him . . .
. . . .
Woburn story . . . getting on . . . finish it . . . then
. . . .
sleep . . . no more stories . . . no more words . . .
. . . .
come on . . . next thing . . . he—
. . . .

OPENER (*with* VOICE *and* MUSIC): And I close.

Silence.

I start again.

VOICE:—down . . . gentle slope . . . boreen . . . giant aspens . . . wind in the boughs . . . faint sea . . . Woburn . . . same old coat . . . he goes on . . . stops . . . not a soul . . . not yet . . . night too bright . . . say what you like . . . the bank . . . he hugs the bank . . . same old stick . . . he goes down . . . falls . . . on purpose or not . . . can't see . . . he's down . . . that's what counts . . . face in the mud . . . arms spread . . . that's the idea . . . already . . . we're there already . . . no not yet . . . he gets up . . . knees first . . . hands flat . . . in the mud . . . head sunk . . . then up . . . on his feet . . . huge bulk . . . come on . . . he goes on . . . he goes down . . . come on . . . in his head . . . what's in his head . . . a hole . . . a shelter . . . a hollow . . . in the dunes . . . a cave . . . vague memory . . . in his head . . . of a cave . . . he goes down . . . no more trees . . . no more bank . . . he's changed . . . not enough . . . night too bright . . . soon the dunes . . . no more cover . . . he stops . . . not a soul . . . not—

Silence.

MUSIC: . . . .

Silence.

VOICE ⎫
MUSIC ⎭ (*together*):   —rest . . . sleep . . . no more stories
. . . .
. . . no more words . . . don't give up . . . it's the right
. . . .
one . . . we're there . . . nearly . . . I'm there . . .
. . . .
somewhere . . . Woburn . . . I've got him . . . don't
. . . .
lose him . . . follow him . . . to the end . . . come on
. . . .

. . . this time . . . it's the right one . . . finish . . . sleep

. . . .

. . . Woburn . . . come on—

. . . .

Silence.

OPENER: So, at will.
They say, It's in his head.
It's not. I open.

VOICE:—falls . . . again . . . on purpose or not . . . can't see
. . . he's down . . . that's what matters . . . face in the
sand . . . arms spread . . . bare dunes . . . not a scrub
. . . same old coat . . . night too bright . . . say what
you like . . . sea louder . . . like thunder . . . manes of
foam . . . Woburn . . . his head . . . what's in his head
. . . peace . . . peace again . . . in his head . . . no
further . . . to go . . . to seek . . . sleep . . . no . . .
not yet . . . he gets up . . . knees first . . . hands flat . . .
in the sand . . . head sunk . . . then up . . . on his feet
. . . huge bulk . . . same old broad-brim . . . jammed
down . . . come on . . . he's off again . . . ton weight
. . . in the sand . . . knee-deep . . . he goes down . . .
sea—

OPENER (*with* VOICE): And I close.

Silence.

I open the other.

MUSIC: . . . .

OPENER (*with* MUSIC): And I close.

Silence.

So, at will.
It's my life, I live on that.

Pause.

Yes, that's right.

Pause.

What do I open?
They say, He opens nothing, he has nothing to open,
it's in his head.
They don't see me, they don't see what I do, they
don't see what I have, and they say, He opens nothing,
he has nothing to open, it's in his head.
I don't protest any more, I don't say any more, There
is nothing in my head.
I don't answer any more.
I open and close.

VOICE:—lights . . . of the land . . . the island . . . the sky
. . . he need only . . . lift his head . . . his eyes . . . he'd
see them . . . shine on him . . . but no . . . he—

Silence.

MUSIC (*brief*): . . . .

Silence.

OPENER: They say, That is not his life, he does not live on
that. They don't see me, they don't see what my life is,
they don't see what I live on, and they say, That is not
his life, he does not live on that.

Pause.

I have lived on it . . . pretty long.
Long enough.
Listen.

VOICE (*weakening*):—this time . . . I'm there . . . Woburn
. . . it's him . . . I've seen him . . . I've got him . . .

come on . . . same old coat . . . he goes down . . . falls
. . . falls again . . . on purpose or not . . . can't see . . .
he's down . . . that's what counts . . . come on—

OPENER (*with* VOICE): Full strength.

VOICE:—face . . . in the stones . . . no more sand . . . all
stones . . . that's the idea . . . we're there . . . this time
. . . no . . . not yet . . . he gets up . . . knees first . . .
hands flat . . . in the stones . . . head sunk . . . then up
. . . on his feet . . . huge bulk . . . Woburn . . . faster . . .
off again . . . he goes down . . . he—

Silence.

MUSIC (*weakening*): . . . .

OPENER (*with* MUSIC): Full strength.

MUSIC: . . . .

Silence.

OPENER: That's not all.
I open both.
Listen.

VOICE ⎱
MUSIC ⎰ (*together*): —sleep . . . no more searching . . . to
. . . .
find him . . . in the dark . . . to see him . . . to say him
. . . .
. . . for whom . . . that's it . . . no matter . . . never
. . . .
him . . . never right . . . start again . . . in the dark . . .
. . . .
done with that . . . this time . . . it's right . . . we're
. . . .
there . . . nearly . . . finish—
. . . .

Silence.

OPENER: From one world to another, it's as though they drew together.

We have not much further to go.

Good.

VOICE } (*together*): —nearly . . . I've got him . . . I've
MUSIC } . . . .
seen him . . . I've said him . . . we're there . . . nearly
. . . .
. . . no more stories . . . all false . . . this time . . . it's
. . . .
the right one . . . I have it . . . finish it . . . sleep . . .
. . . .
Woburn . . . it's him . . . I've got him . . . follow him
. . . .
. . . to—
. . . .

Silence.

OPENER: Good.

Pause.

Yes, that's right, the month of May.
You know, the reawakening.

Pause.

I open.

VOICE:—no tiller . . . no thwarts . . . no oars . . . afloat . . . sucked out . . . then back . . . aground . . . drags free . . . out . . . Woburn . . . he fills it . . . flat out . . . face in the bilge . . . arms spread . . . same old coat . . . hands clutching . . . the gunnels . . . no . . . I don't know . . . I see him . . . he clings on . . . out to sea . . . heading nowhere . . . for the island . . . then no more . . . else—

Silence.

MUSIC: . . . .

Silence.

OPENER: They said, It's his, it's his voice, it's in his head.

Pause.

VOICE:—faster . . . scudding . . . rearing . . . plunging . . .
heading nowhere . . . for the island . . . then no more
. . . elsewhere . . . anywhere . . . heading anywhere . . .
lights—

Silence.

OPENER: No resemblance.
I answered, And that . . .

MUSIC (*brief*): . . . .

Silence.

OPENER: . . . is that mine too?
But I don't answer any more.
And they don't say anything any more.
They have quit.
Good.

Pause.

Yes, the month of May, that's right, the end of May.
The long days.

Pause.

I open.

Pause.

I'm afraid to open.

But I must open.
So I open.

VOICE:—come on . . . Woburn . . . arms spread . . . same old coat . . . face in the bilge . . . he clings on . . . island astern . . . far astern . . . heading out . . . vast deep . . . no more land . . . his head . . . what's in his head . . . Woburn—

OPENER (*with* VOICE): Come on! Come on!

VOICE:—at last . . . no more coming . . . no more going . . . seeking elsewhere . . . always elsewhere . . . we're there . . . nearly . . . Woburn . . . hang on . . . don't let go . . . lights gone . . . of the land . . . all gone . . . nearly all . . . too far . . . too late . . . of the sky . . . those . . . if you like . . . he need only . . . turn over . . . he'd see them . . . shine on him . . . but no . . . he clings on . . . Woburn . . . he's changed . . . nearly enough—

Silence.

MUSIC: . . . .

OPENER (*with* MUSIC): Good God.

MUSIC: . . . .

Silence.

OPENER: Good God good God.

Pause.

There was a time I asked myself, What is it?
There were times I answered, It's the outing.
Two outings.
Then the return.
Where?
To the village.

To the inn.

Two outings, then at last the return, to the village, to the inn, by the only road that leads there.

An image, like any other.

But I don't answer any more.

I open.

VOICE ⎫
MUSIC ⎭ (*together*): —don't let go . . . finish . . . it's the
. . . .
right one . . . I have it . . . this time . . . we're there . . .
. . . .
Woburn . . . nearly—
. . . .

OPENER (*with* VOICE *and* MUSIC): As though they had joined arms.

VOICE ⎫
MUSIC ⎭ (*together*): —sleep . . . no more stories . . . come
. . . .
on . . . Woburn . . . it's him . . . see him . . . say him
. . . .
. . . to the end . . . don't let go—
. . . .

OPENER (*with* VOICE *and* MUSIC): Good.

VOICE ⎫
MUSIC ⎭ (*together*): —nearly . . . just a few more . . . a
. . . .
few more . . . I'm there . . . nearly . . . Woburn . . .
. . . .
it's him . . . it was him . . . I've got him . . . nearly—
. . . .

OPENER (*with* VOICE *and* MUSIC, *fervently*): Good!

VOICE ⎫
MUSIC ⎭ (*together*): —this time . . . it's right . . . finish . . .
. . . .

no more stories . . . sleep . . . we're there . . . nearly . . .
. . . .
just a few more . . . don't let go . . . Woburn . . . he
. . . .
clings on . . . come on . . . come on—
. . . .

Silence.

Words and Music

a radio play

music by John Beckett

MUSIC: *Small orchestra softly tuning up.*

WORDS: Please! (*Tuning. Louder.*) Please! (*Tuning dies away.*) How much longer cooped up here, in the dark? (*With loathing.*) With you! (*Pause.*) Theme . . . (*Pause.*) Theme . . . sloth. (*Pause. Rattled off, low.*) Sloth is of all the passions the most powerful passion and indeed no passion is more powerful than the passion of sloth, this is the mode in which the mind is most affected and indeed—(*Burst of tuning. Loud, imploring.*) Please! (*Tuning dies away. As before.*) The mode in which the mind is most affected and indeed in no mode is the mind more affected than in this, by passion we are to understand a movement of the soul pursuing or fleeing real or imagined pleasure or pain pleasure or pain real or imagined pleasure or pain, of all these movements and who can number them of all these movements and they are legion sloth is the most urgent and indeed by no movement is the soul more urged than by this by this by this to and from by no movement the soul more urged than by this to and—(*Pause.*) From. (*Pause.*) Listen! (*Distant sound of rapidly shuffling carpet slippers.*) At last! (*Shuffling louder. Burst of tuning.*) Hsst!

Tuning dies away. Shuffling louder. Silence.

CROAK: Joe.

WORDS (*humble*): My Lord.

CROAK: Bob.

MUSIC: *Humble muted adsum.*

CROAK: My comforts! Be friends! (*Pause.*) Bob.

MUSIC: *As before.*

CROAK: Joe.

23

WORDS (*as before*): My Lord.

CROAK: Be friends! (*Pause.*) I am late, forgive. (*Pause.*) The face. (*Pause.*) On the stairs. (*Pause.*) Forgive. (*Pause.*) Joe.

WORDS (*as before*): My Lord.

CROAK: Bob.

MUSIC: *As before.*

CROAK: Forgive. (*Pause.*) In the tower. (*Pause.*) The face. (*Long pause.*) Theme tonight . . . (*Pause.*) Theme tonight . . . love. (*Pause.*) Love. (*Pause.*) My club. (*Pause.*) Joe.

WORDS (*as before*): My Lord.

CROAK: Love. (*Pause. Thump of club on ground.*) Love!

WORDS (*orotund*): Love is of all the passions the most powerful passion and indeed no passion is more powerful than the passion of love. (*Clears throat.*) This is the mode in which the mind is most strongly affected and indeed in no mode is the mind more strongly affected than in this.

Pause.

CROAK: *Rending sigh. Thump of club.*

WORDS (*as before*): By passion we are to understand a movement of the soul pursuing or fleeing real or imagined pleasure or pain. (*Clears throat.*) Of all—

CROAK (*anguished*): Oh!

WORDS (*as before*): Of all these movements then and who can number them and they are legion sloth is the LOVE is the most urgent and indeed by no manner of movement is the soul more urged than by this, to and—

Violent thump of club.

CROAK: Bob.
WORDS: From.

Violent thump of club.

CROAK: Bob!
MUSIC: *As before.*
CROAK: Love!
MUSIC: *Rap of baton on stand. Soft music worthy of fore-going, great expression, with audible groans and prot-estations—"No!" "Please" etc.—from* WORDS. *Pause.*
CROAK (*anguished*): Oh! (*Thump of club.*) Louder!
MUSIC: *Loud rap of baton and as before fortissimo, all ex-pression gone, drowning* WORDS' *protestations.*

Pause.

CROAK: My comforts. (*Pause.*) Joe sweet.
WORDS (*as before*): Arise then and go now the manifest un-answerable—
CROAK: *Groans.*
WORDS: . . . to wit this love what is this love that more than all the cursed deadly or any other of its great movers so moves the soul and soul what is this soul that more than by any of its great movers is by love so moved? (*Clears throat. Prosaic.*) Love of woman, I mean, if that is what my Lord means.
CROAK: Alas!
WORDS: What? (*Pause. Very rhetorical.*) Is love the word? (*Pause. Do.*) Is soul the word? (*Pause. Do.*) Do we mean love, when we say love? (*Pause. Do.*) Soul, when we say soul?
CROAK (*anguished*): Oh! (*Pause.*) Bob dear.
WORDS: Do we? (*With sudden gravity.*) Or don't we?
CROAK (*imploring*): Bob!
MUSIC: *Rap of baton. Love and soul music, with just*

audible protestations—*"No!"* *"Please"* *"Peace"* *etc.*— *from* WORDS.

Pause.

CROAK (*anguished*): Oh! (*Pause.*) My balms! (*Pause.*) Joe.

WORDS (*humble*): My Lord.

CROAK: Bob.

MUSIC: *Adsum as before.*

CROAK: My balms! (*Pause.*) Age. (*Pause.*) Joe. (*Pause. Thump of club.*) Joe!

WORDS (*as before*): My Lord.

CROAK: Age!

Pause.

WORDS (*faltering*): Age is . . . age is when . . . old age I mean . . . if that is what my Lord means . . . is when . . . if you're a man . . . were a man . . . huddled . . . nodding . . . the ingle . . . waiting—

Violent thump of club.

CROAK: Bob. (*Pause.*) Age. (*Pause. Violent thump of club.*) Age!

MUSIC: *Rap of baton. Age music, soon interrupted by violent thump.*

CROAK: Together. (*Pause. Thump.*) Together! (*Pause. Violent thump.*) Together, dogs!

MUSIC: *Long la.*

WORDS (*imploring*): No!

Violent thump.

CROAK: Dogs!

MUSIC: *La.*

WORDS (*trying to sing*): Age is when . . . to a man . . .

MUSIC: *Improvement of above.*

WORDS (*trying to sing this*): Age is when to a man . . .

MUSIC: *Suggestion for following.*

WORDS (*trying to sing this*): Huddled o'er . . . the ingle . . . (*Pause. Violent thump. Trying to sing.*) Waiting for the hag to put the . . . pan . . . in the bed . . .

MUSIC: *Improvement of above.*

WORDS (*trying to sing this*): Waiting for the hag to put the pan in the bed . . .

MUSIC: *Suggestion for following.*

WORDS (*trying to sing this*): And bring the . . . arrowroot . . . (*Pause. Violent thump. As before.*) And bring the toddy . . .

Pause. Tremendous thump.

CROAK: Dogs!

MUSIC: *Suggestion for following.*

WORDS (*trying to sing this*): She comes in the ashes . . . (*Imploring.*) No!

MUSIC: *Repeats suggestion.*

WORDS (*trying to sing this*): She comes in the ashes who loved could not be . . . won or . . .

Pause.

MUSIC: *Repeats end of previous suggestion.*

WORDS (*trying to sing this*): Or won not loved . . . (*wearily*) . . . or some other trouble . . . (*Pause. Trying to sing.*) Comes in the ashes like in that old—

MUSIC: *Interrupts with improvement of this and brief suggestion.*

WORDS (*trying to sing this*): Comes in the ashes like in that old light . . . her face . . . in the ashes . . .

Pause.

CROAK: *Groans.*

MUSIC: *Suggestion for following.*

WORDS (*trying to sing this*): That old moonlight . . . on the earth . . . again.

Pause.

MUSIC: *Further brief suggestion.*

Silence.

CROAK: *Groans.*

MUSIC: *Plays air through alone, then invites* WORDS *with opening, pause, invites again and finally accompanies very softly.*

WORDS (*trying to sing, softly*):

> Age is when to a man
> Huddled o'er the ingle
> Shivering for the hag
> To put the pan in the bed
> And bring the toddy
> She comes in the ashes
> Who loved could not be won
> Or won not loved
> Or some other trouble
> Comes in the ashes
> Like in that old light
> The face in the ashes
> That old starlight
> On the earth again.

Long pause.

CROAK (*murmur*): The face. (*Pause.*) The face. (*Pause.*) The face. (*Pause.*) The face.

MUSIC: *Rap of baton and warmly sentimental, about one minute.*

Pause.

CROAK: The face.

WORDS (*cold*): Seen from above in that radiance so cold and faint . . .

> *Pause.*

MUSIC: *Warm suggestion from above for above.*

WORDS (*disregarding, cold*): Seen from above at such close quarters in that radiance so cold and faint with eyes so dimmed by . . . what had passed, its quite . . . piercing beauty is a little . . .

> *Pause.*

MUSIC: *Renews timidly previous suggestion.*

WORDS (*interrupting, violently*): Peace!

CROAK: My comforts! Be friends!

> *Pause.*

WORDS: . . . blunted. Some moments later however, such are the powers of recuperation at this age, the head is drawn back to a distance of two or three feet, the eyes widen to a stare and begin to feast again. (*Pause.*) What then is seen would have been better seen in the light of day, that is incontestable. But how often has it not, in recent months, how often, at all hours, under all angles, in cloud and shine, been seen, I mean. And there is, is there not, in that clarity of silver . . . that clarity of silver . . . is there not . . . my Lord . . . (*Pause.*) Now and then the rye, swayed by a light wind, casts and withdraws its shadow.

> *Pause.*

CROAK: *Groans.*

WORDS: Leaving aside the features or lineaments proper, matchless severally and in their ordonnance—

CROAK: *Groans.*

WORDS: —flare of the black disordered hair as though spread wide on water, the brows knitted in a groove suggesting pain but simply concentration more likely all things considered on some consummate inner process, the eyes of course closed in keeping with this, the lashes . . . (*pause*) . . . the nose . . . (*pause*) . . . nothing, a little pinched perhaps, the lips . . .

CROAK (*anguished*): Lily!

WORDS: . . . tight, a gleam of tooth biting on the under, no coral, no swell, whereas normally . . .

CROAK: *Groans.*

WORDS: . . . the whole so blanched and still that were it not for the great white rise and fall of the breasts, spreading as they mount and then subsiding to their natural . . . aperture—

MUSIC: *Irrepressible burst of spreading and subsiding music with vain protestations—"Peace!" "No!" "Please!" etc.—from* WORDS. *Triumph and conclusion.*

Pause.

WORDS (*gently expostulatory*): My Lord! (*Pause. Faint thump of club.*) I resume, so wan and still and so ravished away that it seems no more of the earth than Mira in the Whale, at her tenth and greatest magnitude on this particular night and shining coldly down —as we say, looking up. (*Pause.*) Some moments later however, such are the powers—

CROAK (*anguished*): No!

WORDS: —the brows uncloud, the lips part and the eyes . . . (*pause*) . . . the brows uncloud, the nostrils dilate, the lips part and the eyes . . . (*pause*) . . . the lips part, a little colour comes back into the cheeks and the eyes . . . (*reverently*) . . . open. (*Pause.*) Then

down a little way . . . (*Pause. Change to poetic tone.*
Low.)

> Then down a little way
> Through the trash
> To where . . . towards where . . .

Pause.

MUSIC: *Discreet suggestion for above.*
WORDS (*trying to sing this*):

> Then down a little way
> Through the trash
> Towards where . . .

Pause.

MUSIC: *Discreet suggestion for following.*
WORDS (*trying to sing this*):

> All dark no begging
> No giving no words
> No sense no need . . .

Pause.
MUSIC: *More confident suggestion for following.*
WORDS (*trying to sing this*):

> Through the scum
> Down a little way
> To whence one glimpse
> Of that wellhead.

Pause.

MUSIC: *Invites with opening, pause, invites again and*
finally accompanies very softly.
WORDS (*trying to sing, softly*):

> Then down a little way
> Through the trash

Towards where
All dark no begging
No giving no words
No sense no need
Through the scum
Down a little way
To whence one glimpse
Of that wellhead.
(*Pause. Shocked.*) My Lord! (*Sound of club let fall.
As before.*) My Lord! (*Shuffling slippers, with halts.
They die away. Long pause.*) Bob. (*Pause.*) Bob!

MUSIC: *Brief rude retort.*

WORDS: Music. (*Imploring.*) Music!

Pause.

MUSIC: *Rap of baton and statement with elements already
used or wellhead alone.*

Pause.

WORDS: Again. (*Pause. Imploring.*) Again!

MUSIC: *As before or only very slightly varied.*

Pause.

WORDS: *Deep sigh.*

Eh Joe

a television play

Joe, late fifties, grey hair, old dressing-gown, carpet slippers, in his room.

1. Joe seen from behind sitting on edge of bed, intent pose, getting up, going to window, opening window, looking out, closing window, drawing curtain, standing intent.

2. Joe do. (=from behind) going from window to door, opening door, looking out, closing door, locking door, drawing hanging before door, standing intent.

3. Joe do. going from door to cupboard, opening cupboard, looking in, closing cupboard, locking cupboard, drawing hanging before cupboard, standing intent.

4. Joe do. going from cupboard to bed, kneeling down, looking under bed, getting up, sitting down on edge of bed as when discovered, beginning to relax.

5. Joe seen from front sitting on edge of bed, relaxed, eyes closed. Hold, then dolly slowly in to closeup of face. First word of text stops this movement.

Camera

Joe's opening movements followed by camera at constant remove, Joe full length in frame throughout. No need to record room as whole. After this opening pursuit, between first and final close-up of face, camera has nine slight moves in towards face, say four inches each time. Each move is stopped by voice resuming, never camera move and voice together. This would give position of camera when dolly stopped by first word of text as one yard from maximum close-up of face. Camera does not move between paragraphs till clear that pause (say three seconds) longer than between phrases. Then four inches in say four seconds when movement stopped by voice resuming.

35

Voice

   Low, distinct, remote, little colour, absolutely steady rhythm, slightly slower than normal. Between phrases a beat of one second at least. Between paragraphs about seven, i.e., three before camera starts to advance and four for advance before it is stopped by voice resuming.

Face

   Practically motionless throughout, eyes unblinking during paragraphs, impassive except in so far as it reflects mounting tension of listening. Brief zones of relaxation between paragraphs when perhaps voice has relented for the evening and intentness may relax variously till restored by voice resuming.

WOMAN'S VOICE:
   Joe . . .
   (*Eyes open, resumption of intentness.*)
   Joe . . .
   (*Full intentness.*)
   Thought of everything? . . . Forgotten nothing? . . . You're all right now, eh? . . . No one can see you now . . . No one can get at you now . . . Why don't you put out that light? . . . There might be a louse watching you . . . Why don't you go to bed? . . . What's wrong with that bed, Joe? . . . You changed it, didn't you? . . . Made no difference? . . . Or is the heart already? . . . Crumbles when you lie down in the dark . . . Dry rotten at last . . . Eh Joe?

Camera move 1

   The best's to come, you said, that last time . . . Hurrying me into my coat . . . Last I was favoured with from

you . . . Say it you now, Joe, no one'll hear you . . .
Come on, Joe, no one can say it like you, say it again
now and listen to yourself . . . The best's to come . . .
You were right for once . . . In the end.

Camera move 2

You know that penny farthing hell you call your mind
. . . That's where you think this is coming from, don't
you? . . . That's where you heard your father . . . Isn't
that what you told me? . . . Started in on you one
June night and went on for years . . . On and off . . .
Behind the eyes . . . That's how you were able to
throttle him in the end . . . Mental thuggee you called
it . . . One of your happiest fancies . . . Mental thuggee
. . . Otherwise he'd be plaguing you yet . . . Then your
mother when her hour came . . . "Look up, Joe, look
up, we're watching you" . . . Weaker and weaker till
you laid her too . . . Others . . . All the others . . . Such
love he got . . . God knows why . . . Pitying love . . .
None to touch it . . . And look at him now . . . Throt-
tling the dead in his head.

Camera move 3

Anyone living love you now, Joe? . . . Anyone living
sorry for you now? . . . That slut that comes on Satur-
day, you pay her, don't you? . . . Penny a hoist tup-
pence as long as you like . . . Watch yourself you
don't run short, Joe . . . Ever think of that? . . . Eh
Joe? . . . What it'd be if you ran out of us . . . Not
another soul to still . . . Sit there in his stinking old
wrapper hearing himself . . . That lifelong adorer . . .
Weaker and weaker till not a gasp left there either . . .

Is it that you want? . . . Well preserved for his age and the silence of the grave . . . That old paradise you were always harping on . . . No Joe . . . Not for the likes of you.

Camera move 4

I was strong myself when I started . . . In on you . . . Wasn't I, Joe? . . . Normal strength . . . Like those summer evenings in the Green . . . In the early days . . . Of our idyll . . . When we sat watching the ducks . . . Holding hands exchanging vows . . . How you admired my elocution! . . . Among other charms . . . Voice like flint glass . . . To borrow your expression . . . Powerful grasp of language you had . . . Flint glass . . . You could have listened to it for ever . . . And now this . . . Squeezed down to this . . . How much longer would you say? . . . Till the whisper . . . You know . . . When you can't hear the words . . . Just the odd one here and there . . . That's the worst . . . Isn't it, Joe? . . . Isn't that what you told me . . . Before we expire . . . The odd word . . . Straining to hear . . . Why is that, Joe? . . . Why must you do that? . . . When you're nearly home . . . What matter then . . . What we mean . . . It should be the best . . . Nearly home again . . . Another stilled . . . And it's the worst . . . Isn't that what you said? . . . The whisper . . . The odd word . . . Straining to hear . . . Brain tired squeezing . . . It stops in the end . . . You stop it in the end . . . Imagine if you couldn't . . . Ever think of that? . . . If it went on . . . The whisper in your head . . . Me whispering at you in your head . . . Things you can't catch . . . On and off . . . Till you join us . . . Eh Joe?

Camera move 5

How's your Lord these days? . . . Still worth having?
. . . Still lapping it up? . . . The passion of our Joe . . .
Wait till He starts talking to you . . . When you're
done with yourself . . . All your dead dead . . . Sitting
there in your foul old wrapper . . . Very fair health for
a man of your years . . . Just that lump in your bubo
. . . Silence of the grave without the maggots . . . To
crown your labours . . . Till one night . . . "Thou fool
thy soul" . . . Put your thugs on that . . . Eh Joe? . . .
Ever think of that? . . . When He starts in on you . . .
When you're done with yourself . . . If you ever are.

Camera move 6

Yes, great love God knows why . . . Even me . . . But
I found a better . . . As I hope you heard . . . Preferable
in all respects . . . Kinder . . . Stronger . . . More in-
telligent . . . Better looking . . . Cleaner . . . Truthful
. . . Faithful . . . Sane . . . Yes . . . I did all right.

Camera move 7

But there was one didn't . . . You know the one I
mean, Joe . . . The green one . . . The narrow one . . .
Always pale . . . The pale eyes . . . Spirit made light
. . . To borrow your expression . . . The way they
opened after . . . Unique . . . Are you with me now?
. . . Eh Joe? . . . There was love for you . . . The best's
to come, you said . . . Bundling her into her Avoca
sack . . . Her fingers fumbling with the big horn but-
tons . . . Ticket in your pocket for the first morning
flight . . . You've had her, haven't you? . . . You've
laid her? . . . Of course he has . . . She went young
. . . No more old lip from her.

Camera move 8

Ever know what happened? . . . She didn't say? . . .
Just the announcement in the *Independent* . . . "On
Mary's beads we plead her needs and in the Holy
Mass" . . . Will I tell you? . . . Not interested? . . .
Well I will just the same . . . I think you should know
. . . That's right, Joe, squeeze away . . . Don't lose
heart now . . . When you're nearly home . . . I'll
soon be gone . . . The last of them . . . Unless that
poor slut loves you . . . Then yourself . . . That old
bonfire . . . Years of that stink . . . Then the silence
. . . A dollop of that . . . To crown all . . . Till His Nibs
. . . One dirty winter night . . . "Mud thou art."

Camera move 9

All right . . . Warm summer night . . . All sleeping . . .
Sitting on the edge of her bed in her lavender slip . . .
You know the one . . . Ah she knew you, heavenly
powers! . . . Faint lap of sea through open window . . .
Gets up in the end and slips out as she is . . . Moon . . .
Stock . . . Down the garden and under the viaduct . . .
Sees from the seaweed the tide is flowing . . . Goes on
down to the edge and lies down with her face in the
wash . . . Cut a long story short doesn't work . . . Gets
up in the end sopping wet and back up to the house
. . . Gets out the Gillette . . . The make you recom-
mended for her body hair . . . Back down the garden
and under the viaduct . . . Takes the blade from the
holder and lies down at the edge on her side . . . Cut
another long story short doesn't work either . . . You
know how she always dreaded pain . . . Tears a strip
from the slip and ties it round the scratch . . . Gets up
in the end and back up to the house . . . Slip clinging

the way wet silk will . . . This all new to you, Joe? . . .
Eh Joe? . . . Gets the tablets and back down the
garden and under the viaduct . . . Takes a few on the
way . . . Unconscionable hour by now . . . Moon going
off the shore behind the hill . . . Stands a bit looking
at the beaten silver . . . Then starts along the edge to
a place further down near the Rock . . . Imagine what
in her mind to make her do that . . . Imagine . . .
Trailing her feet in the water like a child . . . Takes a
few more on the way . . . Will I go on, Joe? . . . Eh
Joe? . . . Lies down in the end with her face a few feet
from the tide . . . Clawing at the shingle now . . . Has
it all worked out this time . . . Finishes the tube . . .
There's love for you . . . Eh Joe? . . . Scoops a little
cup for her face in the stones . . . The green one . . .
The narrow one . . . Always pale . . . The pale eyes . . .
The look they shed before . . . The way they opened
after . . . Spirit made light . . . Wasn't that your description, Joe? . . . (*Voice drops to whisper, almost in-
audible except words in italics.*) All right . . . You've
had the best . . . Now *imagine* . . . Before she goes . . .
Face in the cup . . . Lips on a *stone* . . . Taking Joe
with her . . . Light gone . . . *"Joe Joe"* . . . No sound
. . . To the *stones* . . . Say it now, no one'll hear
you . . . Say "Joe" it parts the *lips* . . . *Imagine* the
hands . . . The *solitaire* . . . Against a *stone* . . . Imagine
the *eyes* . . . Spiritlight . . . Month of June . . . What
year of your Lord? . . . *Breasts* in the stones . . . And
the *hands* . . . Before they go . . . *Imagine* the hands
. . . What are they at? . . . In the *stones* . . . (*Image
fades, voice as before.*) What are they fondling? . . .
Till they go . . . *There's love for you* . . . Isn't it, Joe?
. . . Wasn't it, Joe? . . . *Eh Joe?* . . . Wouldn't you say?
. . . Compared to us . . . Compared to Him . . . *Eh
Joe?* (*Voice and image out.*)

Play

a stage play

Characters

w1 First Woman
w2 Second Woman
m   Man

Front centre, touching one another, three identical grey urns (see page 63) about one yard high. From each a head protrudes, the neck held fast in the urn's mouth. The heads are those, from left to right as seen from auditorium, of w2, m, and w1. They face undeviatingly front throughout the play. Faces so lost to age and aspect as to seem almost part of urns. But no masks.

Their speech is provoked by a spotlight projected on faces alone. See page 62.

The transfer of light from one face to another is immediate. No blackout, i.e., return to almost complete darkness of opening, except where indicated.

The response to light is not quite immediate. At every solicitation a pause of about one second before utterance is achieved, except where a longer delay is indicated.

Faces impassive throughout. Voices toneless except where an expression is indicated.

Rapid tempo throughout.

The curtain rises on a stage in almost complete darkness. Urns just discernible. Five seconds.

Faint spots simultaneously on three faces. Three seconds. Voices faint, largely unintelligible.

45

w1

Yes, strange, darkness best, and the darker the worse, till all dark, then all well, for the time, but it will come, the time will come, the thing is there, you'll see it, get off me, keep off me, all dark, all still, all over, wiped out——

w2

Yes, perhaps, a shade gone, I suppose, some might say, poor thing, a shade gone, just a shade, in the head—(*faint wild laugh*)—just a shade, but I doubt it, *I* doubt it, not really, I'm all right, still all right, do my best, all I can——

Together.
See page
62

M

Yes, peace, one assumed, all out, all the pain, all as if . . . never been, it will come —(*hiccup*)—pardon, no sense in this, oh I know . . . none the less, one assumed, peace . . . I mean . . . not merely all over, but as if . . . never been——

Spots off. Blackout. Five seconds. Strong spots simultaneously on three faces. Three seconds. Voices normal strength.

w1
w2   *Together.*
M

I said to him, Give her up——
One morning as I was sitting——
We were not long together——

Spots off. Blackout. Five seconds. Spot on w1.

w1: I said to him, Give her up. I swore by all I held most sacred——

Spot from w1 *to* w2.

w2: One morning as I was sitting stitching by the open window she burst in and flew at me. Give him up, she screamed, he's mine. Her photographs were kind to her. Seeing her now for the first time full length and in the flesh I understood why he preferred me.

Spot from w2 *to* M.

M: We were not long together when she smelled the rat. Give up that whore, she said, or I'll cut my throat— (*hiccup*) pardon—so help me God. I knew she could have no proof. So I told her I did not know what she was talking about.

Spot from M *to* w2.

w2: What are you talking about? I said, stitching away. Someone yours? Give up whom? I smell you off him, she screamed, he stinks of bitch.

Spot from w2 *to* w1.

w1: Though I had him dogged for months by a first-rate man, no shadow of proof was forthcoming. And there was no denying that he continued as . . . assiduous as ever. This, and his horror of the merely Platonic thing, made me sometimes wonder if I were not accusing him unjustly. Yes.

Spot from w1 *to* M.

M: What have you to complain of? I said. Have I been neglecting you? How could we be together in the way we are if there were someone else? Loving her as I did, with all my heart, I could not but feel sorry for her.

Spot from M *to* w2.

w2: Fearing she was about to offer me violence I rang for Erskine and had her shown out. Her parting words, as he could testify, if he is still alive, and has not forgotten, coming and going on the earth, letting people in, showing people out, were to the effect that she would settle my hash. I confess this did alarm me a little, at the time.

Spot from w2 *to* m.

m: She was not convinced. I might have known. I smell her off you, she kept saying. There was no answer to this. So I took her in my arms and swore I could not live without her. I meant it, what is more. Yes, I am sure I did. She did not repulse me.

Spot from m *to* w1.

w1: Judge then of my astoundment when one fine morning, as I was sitting stricken in the morning room, he slunk in, fell on his knees before me, buried his face in my lap and . . . confessed.

Spot from w1 *to* m.

m: She put a bloodhound on me, but I had a little talk with him. He was glad of the extra money.

Spot from m *to* w2.

w2: Why don't you get out, I said, when he started moaning about his home life, there is obviously nothing between you any more. Or is there?

Spot from w2 *to* w1.

w1: I confess my first feeling was one of wonderment. What a male!

Spot from w1 *to* m. *He opens his mouth to speak.*
Spot from m *to* w2.

w2: Anything between us, he said, what do you take me for, a something machine? And of course with him no danger of the . . . spiritual thing. Then why don't you get out? I said. I sometimes wondered if he was not living with her for her money.

Spot from w2 *to* m.

m: The next thing was the scene between them. I can't have her crashing in here, she said, threatening to take my life. I must have looked incredulous. Ask Erskine, she said, if you don't believe me. But she threatens to take her own, I said. Not yours? she said. No, I said, hers. We had fun trying to work this out.

Spot from m *to* w1.

w1: Then I forgave him. To what will love not stoop! I suggested a little jaunt to celebrate, to the Riviera or our darling Grand Canary. He was looking pale. Peaked. But this was not possible just then. Professional commitments.

Spot from w1 *to* w2.

w2: She came again. Just strolled in. All honey. Licking her lips. Poor thing. I was doing my nails, by the open window. He has told me all about it, she said. Who he, I said filing away, and what it? I know what torture you must be going through, she said, and I have dropped in to say I bear you no ill-feeling. I rang for Erskine.

Spot from w2 *to* m.

m: Then I got frightened and made a clean breast of it. She was looking more and more desperate. She had a razor in her vanity-bag. Adulterers, take warning, never admit.

Spot from m *to* w1.

w1: When I was satisfied it was all over I went to have a gloat. Just a common tart. What he could have found in her when he had me——

Spot from w1 *to* w2.

w2: When he came again we had it out. I felt like death. He went on and on about why he had to tell her. Too risky and so on. That meant he had gone back to her. Back to that!

Spot from w2 *to* w1.

w1: Pudding face, puffy, spots, blubber mouth, jowls, no neck, dugs you could——

Spot from w1 *to* w2.

w2: He went on and on. I could hear a mower. An old hand mower. I stopped him and said that whatever I might feel I had no silly threats to offer—but not much stomach for her leavings either. He thought that over for a bit.

Spot from w2 *to* w1.

w1: Calves like a flunkey—

Spot from w1 *to* m.

m: When I saw her again she knew. She was looking—(*hiccup*)—wretched. Pardon. Some fool was cutting grass. A little rush, then another. The problem was how to convince her that no . . . revival of intimacy was involved. I couldn't. I might have known. So I

took her in my arms and said I could not go on living
without her. I don't believe I could have.

Spot from M *to* W2.

w2: The only solution was to go away together. He swore
we should as soon as he had put his affairs in order.
In the meantime we were to carry on as before. By
that he meant as best we could.

Spot from W2 *to* W1.

w1: So he was mine again. All mine. I was happy again.
I went about singing. The world——

Spot from W1 *to* M.

M: At home all heart to heart, new leaf and bygones
bygones. I ran into your ex-doxy, she said one night,
on the pillow, you're well out of that. Rather uncalled
for, I thought. I am indeed, sweetheart, I said, I am
indeed. God what vermin women. Thanks to you,
angel, I said.

Spot from M *to* W1.

w1: Then I began to smell her off him again. Yes.

Spot from W1 *to* W2.

w2: When he stopped coming I was prepared. More or
less.

Spot from W2 *to* M.

M: Finally it was all too much. I simply could no
longer——

Spot from M *to* W1.

w1: Before I could do anything he disappeared. That
meant she had won. That slut! I couldn't credit it. I

lay stricken for weeks. Then I drove over to her place. It was all bolted and barred. All grey with frozen dew. On the way back by Ash and Snodland——

Spot from w1 *to* M.

M: I simply could no longer——

Spot from M *to* w2.

w2: I made a bundle of his things and burnt them. It was November and the bonfire was going. All night I smelt them smouldering.

Spot off w2. *Blackout. Five seconds. Spots half previous strength simultaneously on three faces. Three seconds. Voices proportionately lower.*

w1		Mercy, mercy——
w2	*Together.*	To say I am——
M		When first this change——

Spots off. Blackout. Five seconds. Spot on M.

M: When first this change I actually thanked God. I thought, It is done, it is said, now all is going out——

Spot from M *to* w1.

w1: Mercy, mercy, tongue still hanging out for mercy. It will come. You haven't seen me. But you will. Then it will come.

Spot from w1 *to* w2.

w2: To say I am not disappointed, no, I am. I had anticipated something better. More restful.

Spot from w2 *to* w1.

w1: Or you will weary of me. Get off me.

Spot from w1 *to* M.

M: Down, all going down, into the dark, peace is coming, I thought, after all, at last, I was right, after all, thank God, when first this change.

Spot from M *to* w2.

w2: Less confused. Less confusing. At the same time I prefer this to . . . the other thing. Definitely. There are endurable moments.

Spot from w2 *to* M.

M: I thought.

Spot from M *to* w2.

w2: When you go out—and I go out. Some day you will tire of me and go out . . . for good.

Spot from w2 *to* w1.

w1: Hellish half-light.

Spot from w1 *to* M.

M: Peace, yes, I suppose, a kind of peace, and all that pain as if . . . never been.

Spot from M *to* w2.

w2: Give me up, as a bad job. Go away and start poking and pecking at someone else. On the other hand——

Spot from w2 *to* w1.

w1: Get off me! (*Vehement.*) Get off me!

Spot from w1 *to* M.

M: It will come. Must come. There is no future in this.

Spot from M *to* w2.

w2: On the other hand things may disimprove, there is that danger.

Spot from w2 *to* M.

M: Oh of course I know now——

Spot from M *to* w1.

w1: Is it that I do not tell the truth, is that it, that some day somehow I may tell the truth at last and then no more light at last, for the truth?

Spot from w1 *to* w2.

w2: You might get angry and blaze me clean out of my wits. Mightn't you?

Spot from w2 *to* M.

M: I know now, all that was just . . . play. And all this? When will all this——

Spot from M *to* w1.

w1: Is that it?

Spot from w1 *to* w2.

w2: Mightn't you?

Spot from w2 *to* M.

M: All this, when will all this have been . . . just play?

Spot from M *to* w1.

w1: I can do nothing . . . for anybody . . . any more . . . thank God. So it must be something I have to say. How the mind works still!

Spot from w1 *to* w2.

w2: But I doubt it. It would not be like you somehow. And you must know I am doing my best. Or don't you?

Spot from w2 *to* m.

m: Perhaps they have become friends. Perhaps sorrow——

Spot from m *to* w1.

w1: But I have said all I can. All you let me. All I——

Spot from w1 *to* m.

m: Perhaps sorrow has brought them together.

Spot from m *to* w2.

w2: No doubt I make the same mistake as when it was the sun that shone, of looking for sense where possibly there is none.

Spot from w2 *to* m.

m: Perhaps they meet, and sit, over a cup of that green tea they both so loved, without milk or sugar, not even a squeeze of lemon——

Spot from m *to* w2.

w2: Are you listening to me? Is anyone listening to me? Is anyone looking at me? Is anyone bothering about me at all?

Spot from w2 *to* m.

m: Not even a squeeze of——

Spot from m *to* w1.

w1: Is it something I should do with my face, other than utter? Weep?

Spot from w1 *to* w2.

w2: Am I taboo, I wonder. Not necessarily, now that all danger is averted. That poor creature—I can hear her —that poor creature——

Spot from w2 *to* w1.

w1: Bite off my tongue and swallow it? Spit it out? Would that placate you? How the mind works still to be sure!

Spot from w1 *to* m.

m: Meet, and sit, now in the one dear old place, now in the other, and sorrow together, and compare— (*hiccup*) pardon—happy memories.

Spot from m *to* w1.

w1: If only I could think, There is no sense in this . . . either, none whatsoever. I can't.

Spot from w1 *to* w2.

w2: That poor creature who tried to seduce you, whatever became of her, do you suppose?—I can hear her. Poor thing.

Spot from w2 *to* m.

m: Personally I always preferred Lipton's.

Spot from m *to* w1.

w1: And that all is falling, all fallen, from the beginning, on empty air. Nothing being asked at all. No one asking me for anything at all.

Spot from w1 *to* w2.

w2: They might even feel sorry for me, if they could see me. But never so sorry as I for them.

Spot from w2 *to* w1.

w1: I can't.

Spot from w1 *to* w2.

w2: Kissing their sour kisses.

Spot from w2 *to* M.

M: I pity them in any case, yes, compare my lot with theirs, however blessed, and——

Spot from M *to* w1.

w1: I can't. The mind won't have it. It would have to go. Yes.

Spot from w1 *to* M.

M: Pity them.

Spot from M *to* w2.

w2: What do you do when you go out? Sift?

Spot from w2 *to* M.

M: Am I hiding something? Have I lost——

Spot from M *to* w1.

w1: She had means, I fancy, though she lived like a pig.

Spot from w1 *to* w2.

w2: Like dragging a great roller, on a scorching day. The strain . . . to get it moving, momentum coming——

Spot off w2. *Blackout. Three seconds. Spot on* w2.

w2: Kill it and strain again.

Spot from w2 *to* M.

M: Have I lost . . . the thing you want? Why go out? Why go——

Spot from M *to* w2.

w2: And you perhaps pitying me, thinking, Poor thing, she needs a rest.

Spot from w2 *to* w1.

w1: Perhaps she has taken him away to live . . . somewhere in the sun.

Spot from w1 *to* M.

M: Why go down? Why not—

Spot from M *to* w2.

w2: I don't know.

Spot from w2 *to* w1.

w1: Perhaps she is sitting somewhere, by the open window, her hands folded in her lap, gazing down out over the olives——

Spot from w1 *to* M.

M: Why not keep on glaring at me without ceasing? I might start to rave and—(*hiccup*)—bring it up for you. Par——

Spot from M *to* w2.

w2: No.

Spot from w2 *to* M.

M: —don.

Spot from M *to* w1.

w1: Gazing down out over the olives, then the sea, wonder-
ing what can be keeping him, growing cold. Shadow
stealing over everything. Creeping. Yes.

Spot from w1 *to* m.

m: To think we were never together.

Spot from m *to* w2.

w2: Am I not perhaps a little unhinged already?

Spot from w2 *to* w1.

w1: Poor creature. Poor creatures.

Spot from w1 *to* m.

m: Never woke together, on a May morning, the first to
wake to wake the other two. Then in a little
dinghy——

Spot from m *to* w1.

w1: Penitence, yes, at a pinch, atonement, one was re-
signed, but no, that does not seem to be the point
either.

Spot from w1 *to* w2.

w2: I say, Am I not perhaps a little unhinged already?
(*Hopefully.*) Just a little? (*Pause.*) I doubt it.

Spot from w2 *to* m.

m: A little dinghy——

Spot from m *to* w1.

w1: Silence and darkness were all I craved. Well, I get a
certain amount of both. They being one. Perhaps it is
more wickedness to pray for more.

Spot from w1 *to* m.

m: A little dinghy, on the river, I resting on my oars, they lolling on air-cushions in the stern . . . sheets. Drifting. Such fantasies.

Spot from m *to* w1.

w1: Hellish half-light.

Spot from w1 *to* w2.

w2: A shade gone. In the head. Just a shade. I doubt it.

Spot from w2 *to* m.

m: We were not civilized.

Spot from m *to* w1.

w1: Dying for dark—and the darker the worse. Strange.

Spot from w1 *to* m.

m: Such fantasies. Then. And now——

Spot from m *to* w2.

w2: I doubt it.

Pause. Peal of wild laughter from w2 *cut short as spot from her to* w1.

w1: Yes, and the whole thing there, all there, staring you in the face. You'll see it. Get off me. Or weary.

Spot from w1 *to* m.

m: And now, that you are . . . mere eye. Just looking. At my face. On and off.

Spot from m *to* w1.

w1: Weary of playing with me. Get off me. Yes.

Spot from w1 *to* M.

M: Looking for something. In my face. Some truth. In my eyes. Not even.

Spot from M *to* w2. *Laugh as before from* w2 *cut short as spot from her to* M.

M: Mere eye. No mind. Opening and shutting on me. Am I as much——

Spot off M. *Blackout. Three seconds. Spot on* M.

M: Am I as much as . . . being seen?

Spot off M. *Blackout. Five seconds. Faint spots simultaneously on three faces. Three seconds. Voices faint, largely unintelligible.*

w1 ⎤
w2 ⎬ *Together.* ⎰ Yes, strange, etc.
M ⎦   ⎱ Yes, perhaps, etc.
             Yes, peace, etc.

Repeat play.

M (*closing repeat*): Am I as much as . . . being seen?

Spot off M. *Blackout. Five seconds. Strong spots simultaneously on three faces. Three seconds. Voices normal strength.*

w1 ⎤
w2 ⎬ *Together.* ⎰ I said to him, Give her up——
M ⎦   ⎱ One morning as I was sitting——
             We were not long together——

Spots off. Blackout. Five seconds. Spot on M.

M: We were not long together——

Spot off M. *Blackout. Five seconds.*

Light

The source of light is single and must not be situated outside ideal space (stage) occupied by its victims.

The optimum position for the spot is at the centre of the footlights, the faces being thus lit at close quarters and from below.

When exceptionally three spots are required to light the three faces simultaneously, they should be as a single spot branching into three.

Apart from these moments a single mobile spot should be used, swivelling at maximum speed from one face to another as required.

The method consisting in assigning to each face a separate fixed spot is unsatisfactory in that it is less expressive of a unique inquisitor than the single mobile spot.

Chorus

w1	Yes strange	darkness best	and the darker	the worse
w2	Yes perhaps	a shade gone	I suppose	some might say
M	Yes peace	one assumed	all out	all the pain
w1	till all dark	then all well	for the time	but it will come
w2	poor thing	a shade gone	just a shade	in the head
M	all as if	never been	it will come	(*hiccup*) pardon
w1	the time will come	the thing is there		you'll see it
w2	(*laugh – – – – –*)	just a shade		but I doubt it
M	no sense in this	oh I know		none the less
w1	get off me	keep off me	all dark	all still
w2	*I* doubt it	not really	I'm all right	still all right
M	one assumed	peace I mean	not merely	all over
w1	all over	wiped out——		
w2	do my best	all I can——		
M	but as if	never been——		

62

Urns

In order for the urns to be only one yard high, it is necessary either that traps be used, enabling the actors to stand below stage level, or that they kneel throughout play, the urns being open at the back.

The sitting posture results in urns of unacceptable bulk and is not to be considered.

Come and Go

dramaticule

for John Calder

Characters

FLO
VI } Age undeterminable
RU

Sitting centre side by side stage right to left FLO, VI, *and* RU. *Very erect, facing front, hands clasped in laps.*

Silence.

VI: Ru.

RU: Yes.

VI: Flo.

FLO: Yes.

VI: When did we three last meet?

RU: Let us not speak.

> *Silence.*
> *Exit* VI *right.*
> *Silence.*

FLO: Ru.

RU: Yes.

FLO: What do you think of Vi?

RU: I see little change. (FLO *moves to centre seat, whispers in Ru's ear. Appalled.*) Oh! (*They look at each other.* FLO *puts her finger to her lips.*) Does she not realize?

FLO: God grant not.

> *Enter* VI. FLO *and* RU *turn back front, resume pose.* VI *sits right. Silence.*

FLO: Just sit together as we used to, in the playground at Miss Wade's.

67

RU: On the log.

> *Silence.*
> *Exit* FLO *left.*
> *Silence.*

RU: Vi.
VI: Yes.
RU: How do you find Flo?
VI: She seems much the same. (RU *moves to centre seat, whispers in Vi's ear. Appalled.*) Oh! (*They look at each other.* RU *puts her finger to her lips.*) Has she not been told?
RU: God forbid.

> *Enter* FLO. RU *and* VI *turn back front, resume pose.* FLO *sits left. Silence.*

RU: Holding hands . . . that way.
FLO: Dreaming of . . . love.

> *Silence.*
> *Exit* RU *right.*
> *Silence.*

VI: Flo.
FLO: Yes.
VI: How do you think Ru is looking?
FLO: One sees little in this light. (VI *moves to centre seat, whispers in Flo's ear. Appalled.*) Oh! (*They look at each other.* VI *puts her finger to her lips.*) Does she not know?
VI: Please God not.

> *Enter* RU. VI *and* FLO *turn back front, resume pose.* RU *sits right. Silence.*

VI: May we not speak of the old days? (*Silence.*) Of what

came after? (*Silence.*) Shall we hold hands in the old way?

After a moment they join hands as follows: Vi's right hand with Ru's right hand, Vi's left hand with Flo's left hand, Flo's right hand with Ru's left hand, Vi's arms being above Ru's left arm and Flo's right arm. The three pairs of clasped hands rest on the three laps. Silence.

FLO: I can feel the rings.

Silence.

NOTES

Successive positions

1	Flo	Vi	Ru
2	{ Flo		Ru
	{	Flo	Ru
3	Vi	Flo	Ru
4	{ Vi		Ru
	{ Vi	Ru	
5	Vi	Ru	Flo
6	{ Vi		Flo
	{	Vi	Flo
7	Ru	Vi	Flo

Hands

R u V i Flo

Lighting
Soft, from above only and concentrated on playing area. Rest of stage as dark as possible.

Costume
Full-length coats, buttoned high, dull violet (RU), dull red (VI), dull yellow (FLO). Drab nondescript hats with enough brim to shade faces. Apart from colour differentiation three figures as alike as possible. Light shoes with rubber soles. Hands made up to be as visible as possible. No rings apparent.

Seat
Narrow benchlike seat, without back, just long enough to accommodate three figures almost touching. As little visible as possible. It should not be clear what they are sitting on.

Exits
The figures are not seen to go off stage. They should disappear a few steps from lit area. If dark not sufficient to allow this, recourse should be had to screens or drapes as little visible as possible. Exits and entrances slow, without sound of feet.

Ohs
Three very different sounds.

Voices
As low as compatible with audibility. Colourless except for three "ohs" and two lines following.

Film

This is the original project for *Film*. No attempt has been made to bring it into line with the finished work. The one considerable departure from what was imagined concerns the opening sequence in the street. This was first shot as given, then replaced by a simplified version in which only the indispensable couple is retained. For the rest the shooting followed closely the indications of the script.

The film is divided into three parts. 1. The street (about eight minutes). 2. The stairs (about five minutes). 3. The room (about 17 minutes).

General

Esse est percipi.

All extraneous perception suppressed, animal, human, divine, self-perception maintains in being.

Search of non-being in flight from extraneous perception breaking down in inescapability of self-perception.

No truth value attaches to above, regarded as of merely structural and dramatic convenience.

In order to be figured in this situation the protagonist is sundered into object (O) and eye (E), the former in flight, the latter in pursuit.

It will not be clear until the end of film that pursuing perceiver is not extraneous, but self.

Until end of film O is perceived by E from behind and at an angle not exceeding 45°. Convention: O enters *percipi*=experiences anguish of perceivedness, only when this angle is exceeded.

O not in perceivedness:

O in perceivedness:

E is therefore at pains, throughout pursuit, to keep within this "angle of immunity" and only exceeds it (1) inadvertently at beginning of part one when he first sights O, (2) inadvertently at beginning of part two when he follows O into vestibule and (3) deliberately at end of part three when O is cornered. In first two cases he hastily reduces angle.

Throughout first two parts all perception is E's. E is the camera. But in third part there is O's perception of room and contents and at the same time E's continued perception of O. This poses a problem of images which I cannot solve without technical help. See below, note 8.

The film is entirely silent except for the "ssh!" in part one.

Climate of film comic and unreal. O should invite laughter throughout by his way of moving. Unreality of street scene (see notes to this section).

Outline

1. The street

Dead straight. No sidestreets or intersections. Period: about 1929. Early summer morning. Small factory district. Moderate animation of workers going unhurriedly to work. All going in same direction and all in couples. No automobiles. Two bicycles ridden by men with girl passengers (on crossbar). One cab, cantering nag, driver standing brandishing whip. All persons in opening scene to be shown in some way perceiving—one another, an object, a shop window, a poster, etc., i.e., all contentedly in *pércipere* and *percipi*. First view of above is by E motionless and searching with his eyes for O. He may be supposed at street edge of wide (four yards) sidewalk. O finally comes into view hastening blindly along sidewalk, hugging the wall on his left, in opposite direction to all the others. Long dark overcoat (whereas all others in light summer dress) with collar up, hat pulled down over eyes, briefcase in left hand, right hand shielding exposed side of face. He storms along in comic foundered precipitancy. E's searching eye, turning left from street to sidewalk, picks him up at an angle exceeding that of immunity (O's unperceivedness according to convention) (1). O, entering perceivedness, reacts (after just sufficient onward movement for his gait to be established) by halting and cringing aside towards wall. E immediately draws back to close the angle (2) and O, released from perceivedness, hurries on. E lets him get about ten yards ahead and then starts after him (3). Street elements from now on incidental (except for episode of couple) in the sense that only registered in so far as they happen to enter field of pursuing eye fixed on O.

Episode of couple (4). In his blind haste O jostles an elderly couple of shabby genteel aspect, standing on sidewalk, peering together at a newspaper. They should be discovered by E a few yards before collision. The woman is holding a pet monkey under her left arm. E follows O an instant as he hastens blindly on, then registers couple recovering from shock, comes up with them, passes them slightly and halts to observe them (5). Having recovered they turn and look after O, the woman raising a *lorgnon* to her eyes, the man taking off his pince-nez fastened to his coat by a ribbon. They then look at each other, she lowering her *lorgnon*, he resuming his pince-nez. He opens his mouth to vituperate. She checks him with a gesture and soft "sssh!" He turns again, taking off his pince-nez, to look after O. She feels the gaze of E upon them and turns, raising her *lorgnon,* to look at him. Shé nudges her companion who turns back towards her, resuming his pince-nez, follows direction of her gaze and, taking off his pince-nez, looks at E. As they both stare at E the expression gradually comes over their faces which will be that of the flower-woman in the stairs scene and that of O at the end of film, an expression only to be described as corresponding to an agony of perceivedness. Indifference of monkey, looking up into face of its mistress. They close their eyes, she lowering her *lorgnon,* and hasten away in direction of all the others, i.e., that opposed to O and E (6).

E turns back towards O by now far ahead and out of sight. Immediate acceleration of E in pursuit (blurred transit of encountered elements). O comes into view, grows rapidly larger until E settles down behind him at same angle and remove as before. O disappears suddenly through open housedoor on his left. Immediate acceleration of E who comes up with O in vestibule at foot of stairs.

2. Stairs

Vestibule about four yards square with stairs at inner righthand angle. Relation of streetdoor to stairs such that E's first perception of O (E near door, O motionless at foot of stairs, right hand on banister, body shaken by panting) is from an angle a little exceeding that of immunity. O, entering perceivedness (according to convention), transfers right hand from banister to exposed side of face and cringes aside towards wall on his left. E immediately draws back to close the angle and O, released, resumes his pose at foot of stairs, hand on banister. O mounts a few steps (E remaining near door), raises head, listens, redescends hastily backwards and crouches down in angle of stairs and wall on his right, invisible to one descending (7). E registers him there, then transfers to stairs. A frail old woman appears on bottom landing. She carries a tray of flowers slung from her neck by a strap. She descends slowly, with fumbling feet, one hand steadying the tray, the other holding the banister. Absorbed by difficulty of descent she does not become aware of E until she is quite down and making for the door. She halts and looks full at E. Gradually same expression as that of couple in street. She closes her eyes, then sinks to the ground and lies with face in scattered flowers. E lingers on this a moment, then transfers to where O last registered. He is no longer there, but hastening up the stairs. E transfers to stairs and picks up O as he reaches first landing. Bound forwards and up of E who overtakes O on second flight and is literally at his heels when he reaches second landing and opens with key door of room. They enter room together, E turning with O as he turns to lock the door behind him.

3. The room

Here we assume problem of dual perception solved and enter O's perception (8). E must so manoeuvre throughout what follows, until investment proper, that O is always seen from behind, at most convenient remove, and from an angle never exceeding that of immunity, i.e., preserved from perceivedness.

Small barely furnished room (9). Side by side on floor a large cat and small dog. Unreal quality. Motionless till ejected. Cat bigger than dog. On a table against wall a parrot in a cage and a goldfish in a bowl. This room sequence falls into three parts.

1. Preparation of room (occlusion of windows and mir-

ror, ejection of dog and cat, destruction of print, occlusion of parrot and goldfish).

2. Period in rocking-chair. Inspection and destruction of photographs.

3. Final investment of O by E and dénouement.

1. O stands near door with case in hand and takes in room. Succession of images: dog and cat, side by side, staring at him; mirror; window; couch with rug; dog and cat staring at him; parrot and goldfish, parrot staring at him; rocking-chair; dog and cat staring at him. He sets down case, approaches window from side and draws curtain. He turns towards dog and cat, still staring at him, then goes to couch and takes up rug. He turns towards dog and cat, still staring at him. Holding rug before him he approaches mirror from side and covers it with rug. He turns towards parrot and goldfish, parrot still staring at him. He goes to rocking-chair, inspects it from front. Insistent image of curiously carved headrest (10). He turns towards dog and cat still staring at him. He puts them out of room (11). He takes up case and is moving towards chair when rug falls from mirror. He drops case, hastens to wall between couch and mirror, follows walls past window, approaches mirror from side, picks up rug and, holding it before him, covers mirror with it again. He returns to case, picks it up, goes to chair, sits down and is opening case when disturbed by print, pinned to wall before him, of the face of God the Father, the eyes staring at him severely. He sets down case on floor to his left, gets up and inspects print. Insistent image of wall, paper hanging off in strips (10). He tears print from wall, tears it in four, throws down the pieces and grinds them underfoot. He turns back to chair, image again of its curious headrest, sits down, image again of tattered wall-paper, takes case on

his knees, takes out a folder, sets down case on floor to his left and is opening folder when disturbed by parrot's eye. He lays folder on case, gets up, takes off overcoat, goes to parrot, close-up of parrot's eye, covers cage with coat, goes back to chair, image again of headrest, sits down, image again of tattered wall-paper, takes up folder and is opening it when disturbed by fish's eye. He lays folder on case, gets up, goes to fish, close-up of fish's eye, extends coat to cover bowl as well as cage, goes back to chair, image again of headrest, sits down, image again of wall, takes up folder, takes off hat and lays it on case to his left. Scant hair or bald, to facilitate identification of narrow black elastic encircling head.

When O sits up and back his head is framed in headrest which is a narrower extension of backrest. Throughout scene of inspection and destruction of photographs E may be supposed immediately behind chair looking down over O's left shoulder (12).

2. O opens folder, takes from it a packet of photographs (13), lays folder on case and begins to inspect photographs. He inspects them in order 1 to 7. When he has finished with 1 he lays it on his knees, inspects 2, lays it on top of 1, and so on, so that when he has finished inspecting them all 1 will be at the bottom of the pile and 7—or rather 6, for he does not lay down 7—at the top. He gives about six seconds each to 1–4, about twice as long to 5 and 6 (trembling hands). Looking at 6 he touches with forefinger little girl's face. After six seconds of 7 he tears it in four and drops pieces on floor on his left. He takes up 6 from top of pile on his knees, looks at it again for about three seconds, tears it in four and drops pieces on floor to his left. So on for the others, looking at each again for about three seconds before tearing it up. 1 must be on tougher mount for he has difficulty in tearing it across. Straining hands. He finally

succeeds, drops pieces on floor and sits, rocking slightly, hands holding armrests (14).

3. Investment proper. Perception from now on, if dual perception feasible, E's alone, except perception of E by O at end. E moves a little back (image of headrest from back), then starts circling to his left, approaches maximum angle and halts. From this open angle, beyond which he will enter *percipi*, O can be seen beginning to doze off. His visible hand relaxes on armrest, his head nods and falls forward, the rock approaches stillness. E advances, opening angle beyond limit of immunity, his gaze pierces the light sleep and O starts awake. The start revives the rock, immediately arrested by foot to floor. Tension of hand on armrest. Turning his head to right, O cringes away from perceivedness. E draws back to reduce the angle and after a moment, reassured, O turns back front and resumes his pose. The rock resumes, dies down slowly as O dozes off again. E now begins a much wider encirclement. Images of curtained window, walls, and shrouded mirror to indicate his path and that he is not yet looking at O. Then brief image of O seen by E from well beyond the angle of immunity, i.e., from near the table with shrouded bowl and cage. O is now seen to be fast asleep, his head sunk on his chest and his hands, fallen from the armrests, limply dangling. E resumes his cautious approach. Images of shrouded bowl and cage and tattered wall adjoining, with same indication as before. Halt and brief image, not far short of full-face, of O still fast asleep. E advances last few yards along tattered wall and halts directly in front of O. Long image of O, full-face, against ground of headrest, sleeping. E's gaze pierces the sleep, O starts awake, stares up at E. Patch over O's left eye now seen for first time. Rock revived by start, stilled at once by foot to ground. Hands clutch armrests. O half starts from chair, then stiffens, staring up at E. Gradually

that look. Cut to E, of whom this very first image (face only, against ground of tattered wall). It is O's face (with patch) but with very different expression, impossible to describe, neither severity nor benignity, but rather acute *intentness*. A big nail is visible near left temple (patch side). Long image of the unblinking gaze. Cut back to O, still half risen, staring up, with that look. O closes his eyes and falls back in chair, starting off rock. He covers his face with his hands. Image of O rocking, his head in his hands but not yet bowed. Cut back to E. As before. Cut back to O. He sits, bowed forward, his head in his hands, gently rocking. Hold it as the rocking dies down.

NOTES

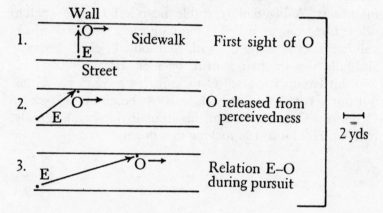

1. First sight of O

2. O released from perceivedness

3. Relation E–O during pursuit

= 2 yds

4. The purpose of this episode, undefendable except as a dramatic convenience, is to suggest as soon as possible unbearable quality of E's scrutiny. Reinforced by episode of flower-woman in stairs sequence.

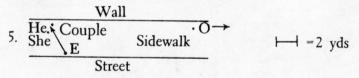

5.

⊢———⊣ = 2 yds

6. Expression of this episode, like that of animals' ejection in part three, should be as precisely stylized as possible. The purpose of the monkey, either unaware of E or indifferent to him, is to anticipate behaviour of animals in part three, attentive to O exclusively.

7. Suggestion for vestibule with (1) O in *percipi* (2) released (3) hiding from flower-woman. Note that even when E exceeds angle of immunity O's face never really seen because of immediate turn aside and (here) hand to shield face.

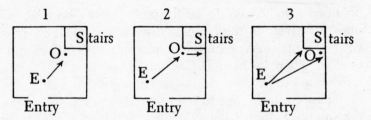

8. Up till now the perceptions of O, hastening *blindly* to illusory sanctuary, have been neglected and must in fact have been negligible. But in the room, until he falls asleep and the investment begins, they must be recorded. And at the same time E's perceiving of O must continue to be given. E is concerned only with O, not with the room, or only incidentally with the room in so far as its elements happen to enter the field of his gaze fastened on O. We see O in the room thanks to E's perceiving and the room itself thanks to O's perceiving. In other words this room sequence, up to the moment of O's falling asleep, is composed of two independent sets of images. I feel that any attempt to express them in simultaneity (composite images, double frame, superimposition, etc.) must prove unsatisfactory. The presentation in a single image of O's perception of the print, for example, and E's perception of O perceiving it—no doubt feasible technically—would per-

$$E \bullet \longrightarrow \underset{O}{\bullet} \longrightarrow \bullet \text{Print}$$

haps make impossible for the spectator a clear apprehension of either. The solution might be in a succession of images of different *quality*, corresponding on the one hand to E's perception of O and on the other to O's perception of the room. This difference of quality might perhaps be sought in different degrees of development, the passage from the one to the other being from greater to lesser and lesser to greater definition or luminosity. The dissimilarity, however obtained, would have to be flagrant. Having been up till now exclusively in the E quality, we would suddenly pass, with O's first survey of the room, into this different O quality. Then back to the E quality when O is shown moving to the window. And so on throughout the sequence, switching from the one to the other as required. Were this the solution adopted it might be desirable to establish, by means of brief sequences, the O quality in parts one and two.

This seems to be the chief problem of the film, though I perhaps exaggerate its difficulty through technical ignorance.

9.

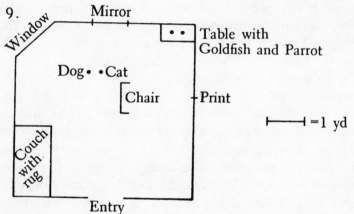

Suggestion for room.

This obviously cannot be O's room. It may be supposed it is his mother's room, which he has not visited for many years and is now to occupy momentarily, to look after the pets, until she comes out of hospital. This has no bearing on the film and need not be elucidated.

10. At close of film face E and face O can only be distinguished (1) by different expressions, (2) by fact of O looking up and E down and (3) by difference of ground

(for O headrest of chair, for E wall). Hence insistence on headrest and tattered wall.

11. Foolish suggestion for eviction of cat and dog. Also see note 6.

Door ————————— •Dog
                •Cat   1

O with dog to door
∘ ←————————
            •Cat   2

Dog out •——→ O back for cat
                   •Cat   3

O with cat to door
→ ←————————
  Dog back   4

Cat out •——→ O back for dog
                •Dog   5

O with dog to door
← ————————
  Cat back   6

Dog out ——→ O back for cat
                •Cat   7

O with cat to door
→ ←————————
  Dog back   8

Cat out —→ O back for dog
                •Dog   9

O with dog to door
∘ ←————————
  Cat back   10

Dog out •——→ O back for cat
                •Cat   11

O with cat to door
←————————
→ Dog back   12

Cat out ——→ O back for dog
                •Dog   13

O with dog to door
————————
→ Cat back   14

Dog out —→ O back for cat
                •Cat   15

O with cat to door
←————————   16

Cat and dog out —→ O picks up case
————————   17

12. Chair from front during photo sequence.

13. Description of photographs.

1. Male infant. Six months. His mother holds him in her arms. Infant smiles front. Mother's big hands. Her severe eyes devouring him. Her big old-fashioned beflowered hat.

2. The same. Four years. On a veranda, dressed in loose nightshirt, kneeling on a cushion, attitude of prayer, hands clasped, head bowed, eyes closed. Half profile. Mother on chair beside him, big hands on knees, head bowed towards him, severe eyes, similar hat to 1.

3. The same. 15 years. Bareheaded. School blazer. Smiling. Teaching a dog to beg. Dog on its hind legs looking up at him.

4. The same. 20 years. Graduation day. Academic gown. Mortar-board under arm. On a platform, receiving scroll from Rector. Smiling. Section of public watching.

5. The same. 21 years. Bareheaded. Smiling. Small moustache. Arm round fiancée. A young man takes a snap of them.

6. The same. 25 years. Newly enlisted. Bareheaded. Uniform. Bigger moustache. Smiling. Holding a little girl in his arms. She looks into his face, exploring it with finger.

7. The same. 30 years. Looking over 40. Wearing hat and overcoat. Patch over left eye. Cleanshaven. Grim expression.

14. Profit by rocking-chair to emotionalize inspection, e.g., gentle steady rock for 1 to 4, rock stilled (foot to ground) after two seconds of 5, rock resumed between 5 and 6, rock stilled after two seconds of 6, rock resumed after 6 and for 7 as for 1–4.

FIRST PERFORMANCES

Eh Joe was first performed on BBC Television on July 4, 1966.

Play was first performed in German at the Ulmer Theater, Ulm-Donau, Germany, on June 14, 1963.

Film was first shown at the Venice Film Festival on September 4, 1965. The first American showing was at the New York Film Festival on September 14, 1965.

Selected Grove Press Paperbacks

17740-1 CRAFTS, KATHY & HAUTHER, BRENDA / How To Beat the System: The Student's Guide to Good Grades / $3.95

17219-1 CUMMINGS, E.E. / 100 Selected Poems / $5.50

17987-0 DURAS, MARGUERITE / Four Novels: The Square; 10:30 on a Summer Night; The Afternoon of Mr. Andesmas; Moderato Cantabile / $9.95

17246-9 DURRENMATT, FRIEDRICH / The Physicists / $6.95

17327-9 FANON, FRANZ / The Wretched of the Earth / $6.95

62073-9 GARWOOD, DARRELL / Under Cover: Thirty-five Years of CIA Deception / $3.95

17390-2 GENET, JEAN / The Maids and Deathwatch: Two Plays / $8.95

17903-X GENET, JEAN / Our Lady of the Flowers / $3.95

62247-2 GERVASI, TOM / America's War Machine: Arsenal of Democracy III / $14.95

17662-6 GERVASI, TOM / Arsenal of Democracy II / $12.95

62345-2 GETTLEMAN, MARVIN, et.al. eds. / El Salvador: Central America in the New Cold War / $12.95

62277-4 GETTLEMAN, MARVIN, et.al., eds. / Vietnam and America: A Documented History / $11.95

17994-3 GIBBS, LOIS MARIE / Love Canal: My Story / $6.95

17648-0 GIRODIAS, MAURICE, ed. / The Olympia Reader / $5.95

17967-9 GOMBROWICZ, WITOLD / Three Novels: Ferdydurke, Pornografia and Cosmos / $12.50

17764-9 GOVER, ROBERT / One Hundred Dollar Misunderstanding / $2.95

62490-4 GUITAR PLAYER MAGAZINE / The Guitar Player Book (Revised and Updated Edition) $11.95

17124-1 HARRIS, FRANK / My Life and Loves / $9.95

17936-6 HARWOOD, RONALD / The Dresser / $5.95

17409-7 HERNTON, CALVIN / Sex and Racism in America / $3.95

17125-X HOCHHUTH, ROLF / The Deputy / $7.95

62115-8 HOLMES, BURTON / The Olympian Games in Athens / $6.95

17075-X INGE, WILLIAM / Four Plays (Come Back, Little Sheba; Picnic; Bus Stop; The Dark at the Top of the Stairs) / $7.95

17209-4 IONESCO, EUGENE / Four Plays (The Bald Soprano, The Lesson, The Chairs, and Jack or The Submission) / $6.95

17226-4 IONESCO, EUGENE / Rhinoceros and Other Plays / $5.95

62123-9 JOHNSON, CHARLES / Oxherding Tale / $6.95

17287-6 KEROUAC, JACK / Mexico City Blues / $7.95

17952-8 KEROUAC, JACK / The Subterraneans / $3.50

62424-6 LAWRENCE, D.H. / Lady Chatterley's Lover / $3.95

17178-0 LESTER, JULIUS / Black Folktales / $4.95

17114-4 MALCOLM X (Breitman., ed.) / Malcolm X Speaks / $6.95

17016-4 MAMET, DAVID / American Buffalo / $5.95

62049-6 MAMET, DAVID / Glengarry Glenn Ross / $6.95

62371-1   MILLER, HENRY / Sexus / $9.95

62375-4   MILLER, HENRY / Tropic of Cancer / $7.95

62053-4   MROZEK, SLAWOMIR / The Elephant / $6.95

62301-1   NAISON, MARK / Communists in Harlem During the Depression / $9.95

13035-6   NERUDA, PABLO / Five Decades: Poems 1925-1970. Bilingual ed. / $14.50

62243-X   NICOSIA, GERALD / Memory Babe: A Critical Biography of Jack Kerouac / $11.95

17092-X   ODETS, CLIFFORD / Six Plays (Waiting for Lefty, Awake and Sing, Golden Boy, Rocket to the Moon, Till the Day I Die, Paradise Lost) / $7.95

17650-2   OE, KENZABURO / A Personal Matter / $6.95

17002-4   OE, KENZABURO / Teach Us To Outgrow Our Madness / $4.95

17992-7   PAZ, OCTAVIO / The Labyrinth of Solitude / $9.95

17084-9   PINTER, HAROLD / Betrayal / $6.95

17232-9   PINTER, HAROLD / The Birthday Party & The Room / $6.95

17251-5   PINTER, HAROLD / The Homecoming / $5.95

17761-4   PINTER, HAROLD / Old Times / $6.95

17539-5   POMERANCE, BERNARD / The Elephant Man / $5.95

17658-8   REAGE, PAULINE / The Story of O, Part II; Return to the Chateau / $3.95

62169-7   RECHY, JOHN / City of Night / $4.50

62171-9   RECHY, JOHN / Numbers / $8.95

13017-8   ROBBE-GRILLET, ALAIN / Djinn (and La Maison de Rendez-Vous) / $8.95

13017-8   ROBBE-GRILLET, ALAIN / The Voyeur / $8.95

62001-1   ROSSET, BARNEY and JORDAN, FRED / Evergreen Review No. 98 / $5.95

62498-X   ROSSET, PETER and VANDERMEER, JOHN / The Nicaragua Reader / $9.95

13012-7   SADE, MARQUIS DE / The 120 Days of Sodom and Other Writings / $14.95

62045-3   SAVONNA, JEANNETTE L. / Jean Genet / $8.95

62495-5   SCHEFFLER, LINDA / Help Thy Neighbor / $7.95

62438-6   SCHNEEBAUM, TOBIAS / Keep the River on Your Right / $12.50

62009-7   SEGALL, J. PETER / Deduct This Book: How Not to Pay Taxes While Ronald Reagan is President / $6.95

17467-4   SELBY, HUBERT / Last Exit to Brooklyn / $3.95

62040-2   SETO, JUDITH ROBERTS / The Young Actor's Workbook / $8.95

17963-3   SHANK, THEODORE / American Alternative Theater / $12.50

17948-X   SHAWN, WALLACE, and GREGORY, ANDRE / My Dinner with Andre / $6.95

62496-3   SIEGAL, FREDERICK, M.D., and MARTA / Aids: The Medical Mystery / $7.95

17887-4   SINGH, KHUSHWANT / Train to Pakistan / $4.50
62446-7   SLOMAN, LARRY / Reefer Madness: Marijuana in America /
$8.95
17797-5   SNOW, EDGAR / Red Star Over China / $9.95
17923-4   STEINER, CLAUDE / Healing Alcoholism / $6.95
17866-1   STOPPARD, TOM / Jumpers / $4.95
13033-X   STOPPARD, TOM / Rosencrantz and Guildenstern Are Dead /
$4.95
17884-X   STOPPARD, TOM / Travesties / $3.95
17230-2   SUZUKI, D.T. / Introduction to Zen Buddhism / $11.95
17224-8   SUZUKI, D.T. / Manual of Zen Buddhism / $7.95
17599-9   THELWELL, MICHAEL / The Harder They Come: A Novel about
Jamaica / $7.95
13020-8   TOOLE, JOHN KENNEDY / A Confederacy of Dunces / $6.95
62168-9   TUTOLA, AMOS / The Palm-Wine Drunkard / $4.50
62189-1   UNGERER, TOMI / Far Out Isn't Far Enough (Illus.) / $12.95
17211-6   WALEY, ARTHUR / Monkey / $8.95
17207-8   WALEY, ARTHUR / The Way and Its Power: A Study of the Tao
Te Ching and Its Place in Chinese Thought / $9.95
17418-6   WATTS, ALAN W. / The Spirit of Zen / $6.95

GROVE PRESS, INC., 920 Broadway, New York, N.Y. 10010